The Story of Croke Park

'This is a brilliant book for any sports fan and an excellent introduction to a beloved Irish landmark and the GAA.'
Irish Independent

'Steeped in the author's love for the venue, the games and indeed Ireland itself, you can almost hear the clash of the ash, the thump of a ball and the roar of the crowd rising from the pages. Hats off to Graham Corcoran too for some stirring and evocative illustrations.'
Irish Examiner

'Who better than the "voice of Gaelic games" himself, Micheál O'Muircheartaigh, to tell *The Story of Croke Park?*'
Evening Echo

'Jam-packed with fascinating facts, this informative book will captivate GAA fans young and old.'
RTEjr

First published 2020 by The O'Brien Press Ltd,
12 Terenure Road East, Rathgar, Dublin 6, D06 HD27, Ireland
Tel: +353 1 4923333; Fax: +353 1 4922777
E-mail: books@obrien.ie
Website: www.obrien.ie
Reprinted 2021.
The O'Brien Press is a member of Publishing Ireland.

ISBN: 978-1-78849-206-5

Photographs courtesy of Croke Park Library and Museum.

7 6 5 4 3 2
23 22 21

Printed and bound by Drukarnia Skleniarz, Poland.
The paper used in this book is produced using pulp from managed forests.

Published in:
DUBLIN
UNESCO
City of Literature

The Story of Croke Park

Micheál Ó Muircheartaigh

illustrated by Graham Corcoran

THE O'BRIEN PRESS
DUBLIN

Contents

My First Visit to Croke Park

It was All Ireland Football Final Day, 26 September 1948. I was standing underneath the Cusack Stand, but closer still to Hill 16. Reigning Champions Cavan were taking on Mayo after an absence of twelve years.

I arrived early and had plenty of time to look at the wonders around about. The pitch, the stands – Hogan, Long and Cusack – and naturally the green box between the Hogan and Long stands from where Michael Ó Hehir broadcast. What a sight.

Nach iontach an mac an saol ar uairibh.

Above all, I recall the almighty gale that blew down the pitch from Canal to Railway end.

THE RAILWAY WALL

Back then, the staunch Railway Wall at the back of Hill 16 would gradually become a viewing area for all it could hold. A few people would come with ladders to the Wall area, charging a very reasonable rate for access.

THE MATCH

Of course the football claimed all the attention once it started: After Tyrone and Dublin in the Minor (won by Tyrone), it was Mayo and Cavan in the Senior.

The score at half time was Cavan 3-3, Mayo 0-0, with two Cavan goals by Tony Tighe, as good as I have ever seen.

'NO HAWKERS ALLOWED'

Upon the shrill of the half-time whistle, ignoring the 'No Hawkers Allowed' signs, a group of ladies raced out onto the pitch, carrying baskets of apples, oranges and other snacks.

The Cusack Stand was their target, and the pace was brisk: the ladies needed to move fast to stay ahead of the stewards.

SECOND HALF

There were four goals for Mayo in the second half, with a pair by the lively Tom Acton, but Cavan's genius Mick Higgins scored one more against the gale in that half hour of wonders.

Mayo really responded to the challenge, and as full-time approached they trailed by a single point. They were then awarded a close-in free at an angle. There was complete silence as the free was taken, and almost instantaneously the silence was shattered as Mick Higgins rose to win possession, securing another All-Ireland win for the Breffni men, with a full-time score of Cavan 4-5, Mayo 4-4.

More than eight goals have never been scored in an All-Ireland Final before or since. What a day; what memories.

Sea, is minic a chuimhním ar an lá úd. Dar liom bhí draíocht mealltach ag baint leis.

Saolú Cumann Lúthchleas Gael – an 'GAA' fadó, fadó …

It may seem strange now, but for a long time Ireland was ruled by Britain. The rules were seldom easy – for example, King Edward declared in the mid-1360s that it was now illegal to play sports like hurling or football!

Sea, nach raibh na rialacha úd dian agus daingean?

This was the way of it until the mid-1800s. Then the ban was lifted, but there was no rush to play sports for a while, as the Irish people were now suffering a terrible famine and poverty.

A NEW ERA

As the worst years of the famine passed, a new era began. On 1 November 1884, seven men met in the Hayes Hotel in Thurles, Co. Tipperary. There, Michael Cusack led the formation of the Gaelic Athletic Association (GAA), created to protect and develop Irish sports – hurling, Gaelic football, athletics and rounders.

Ainmníodh Maurice Davin, lúthchleasaí den scoth, mar Uachtarán; Micheál Cíosóg mar Rúnaí; agus Ard-Easpag Cróc mar Phátrún ar an gCumann nua.

Years later, stands in Croke Park were named in memory of Michael Cusack and Maurice Davin, while the stadium itself was named after Archbishop Croke.

Michael Cusack

GROWTH OF THE GAA

Ever since 1884, the GAA has grown and grown. There are over 2,300 GAA clubs across the thirty-two counties of Ireland, from the two dozen in Longford to the 260 in Cork. There are over 400 more clubs all across the world – from Buenos Aires to Hong Kong, Kuwait to Johannesburg.

The GAA, LGFA and Camogie Association have over half a million members worldwide. They promote Gaelic football, hurling, camogie, handball and rounders, and indirectly the Irish language. Lots of children join their local club before they even start school!

Gur fada buan é Cumann Lúthchleas Gael.

Forbairt ar Áiseanna Imeartha – Development of the Grounds

Croke Park or Páirc an Chrócaigh is Ireland's most famous sporting venue. It's where the GAA's biggest games in hurling, Gaelic football, camogie and ladies' football are played. On big match days, the stands are filled to capacity with over 80,000 followers cheering on their teams, and the atmosphere is extraordinary.

Tugann an dearcadh sin misneach agus dóchas do's na daoine go mórmhór na daoine óga go mbíonn an mian acu 'imirt i bPáirc an Chrócaigh ar lá mór' uair éigin.

THE BATTLE OF CLONTARF

Croke Park is in Drumcondra, Dublin, near the scene of the Battle of Clontarf, a very famous battle. It took place in 1014 AD, between invading Vikings and the Irish forces led by Brian Ború, High King of Ireland.

BUTTERLY'S FIELD

The development of Croke Park began in 1864, when Maurice Butterly rented 21 acres of land south of Clonliffe Road, which became known as 'Butterly's Field'. Back then it would have been surrounded by farms, with cows and sheep grazing close by. Before long the 'Field' became popular for staging events such as running, cycling, football, and even racing small dogs called whippets.

In December 1891, Butterly's Field held its first GAA athletics meeting, with competitions in sports like running, weight throwing and jumping, all of which were very popular.

Bóthar Jones – Jones's Road

In the early years of the GAA, All-Ireland finals in Gaelic football and hurling were played in lots of different venues in Leinster and Munster. Back then, counties were represented by their leading club – not really a county team like we have today. As well as the football and hurling finals, match days usually included the Long Kicking Championship of Ireland and the Poc Fada in hurling.

In 1894, Maurice Butterly sold his sports field. From then on it was known as 'Jones's Road'. The GAA rented playing areas, and the first All-Ireland Finals to be played there were those of 1895, though they were not played until 16 March 1896.

Tipperary won both the football and hurling finals on that day, with Tubberadora defeating Tullaroan of Kilkenny in hurling, and Arravale Rovers beating Pierce O'Mahony's of Meath in football.

A BUSY REFEREE

All four events were refereed by the same person, JJ Kenny of Dublin. *Dhein sé gaisce mór ar an bpáirc an lá úd, ach dhein sé botún amháin* – an error in his score-keeping gave Tipperary a one-point victory when the correct result was a draw.

Having realised that he had erred, JJ later dropped letters by hand to all the Dublin newspapers correcting the mistake. Meath did not seek a replay, and so the case ended there and then.

The like of it has never happened since.

FRANK DINEEN

In 1908, Frank B Dineen bought Jones's Road for £3,250 and put it in trust for the GAA. Dineen also paid for the grass to be re-laid and for terracing to be built for spectators. The Limerick man from Ballylanders is the only person in history to have served as both President and General Secretary of CLG. His contribution to the Association is commemorated in the name of the north stand – now known as Dineen Hill 16.

Páirc Chuimhneacháin an Chrócaigh – Croke Memorial Park

By 1913, the GAA could finally afford to buy Jones's Road from Frank Dineen for the sum of £2,400. From then on it was called Croke Memorial Park, in honour of Archbishop Croke.

A STAND TO STAND IN!

Back in those early days, seating for spectators was not the most comfortable. There were two stands on the Jones's Road side of the ground, and the Long Stand was the better of these two. It had a sloping, rough floor and a corrugated iron roof that slanted towards the pitch. But no seats!

It was possible to climb up onto the roof, and on big match days it was normal to see people being helped up by stewards or even Gardaí so they could get a better view.

Ideas of health and safety had not yet surfaced.

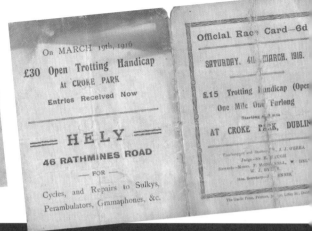

FOUR IN A ROW

Ba é Cluiche Ceannais Peile na bliana 1913 an chéad chluiche a imríodh ar an bPáirc faoin ainm nua, Páirc an Chrócaigh. Ciarraí agus Loch Garman a bhí san iomaíocht.

Kerry won, but who would dream of the wonders ahead for the runners-up? That clash of 1913 was the first of Six All-Ireland Final appearances in a row by the Model County, including winning a wonderful four in a row from 1915 to 1918 in the 'Páirc' that weaves magic.

This was a national record, and though Kerry equalled it on two occasions, it did not 'fall' until Dublin surged to a new high with their fifth in a row in 2019.

Incidentally, Wexford were first to include a priest on a team. Father E Wheeler played on the winning teams of 1915 and 1916, and some people credit his presence with their run of good fortune!

Bíonn cabhair Dé ar an mBóthar.

Réabhlóid – Revolution

Bhí sé tráthúil gur thosnaigh ré nua i saol CLG sa bhliain 1913. Change was needed and it was welcomed.

The years from 1910 to 1920 were very eventful. Europe suffered terribly during the First World War, while Ireland struck for freedom in the Easter Rising of 1916.

In the world of GAA, a national competition for junior inter-county teams began in 1912. In 1913, teams were standardised as fifteen players, parallelograms were painted around the goals and the value of a 'goal' was reduced from five to three points.

16

GAELIC SUNDAY

In 1918, the British Government proclaimed the GAA a 'dangerous organisation'. Gaelic Games without a permit were now banned.

The GAA reacted by organising football games all across Ireland, all starting at 3pm on 4 August of that year.

The day became known as Gaelic Sunday. About 54,000 players took part in those games, and 100,000 spectators turned up to watch. This peaceful protest against the unfair ban succeeded, and the ban was ended.

Caibidil ghonta i stair na tíre a bhí ann agus thug sé ard-mhisneach do mhuintir na tíre. Ní neart go cur le chéile.

Domhnach an Fola – Bloody Sunday

The Irish were still fighting for independence from Britain in 1920. On 21 November of that year, the footballers of Dublin and Tipperary were playing in Croke Park. During the match, a troupe of British soldiers entered the Park. They began to fire at random into the crowd, in retaliation for the killing of fourteen British operatives early that morning. Fourteen people died in Croke Park that day – thirteen spectators and Tipperary footballer Michael Hogan. Hundreds more were wounded.

Ba mhór an slad é in aghaidh daoine a tháinig chun cluiche peile d'fheiscint.

Baisteadh Domhnach na Fola ar an lá, agus maireann a chuimhne fós.

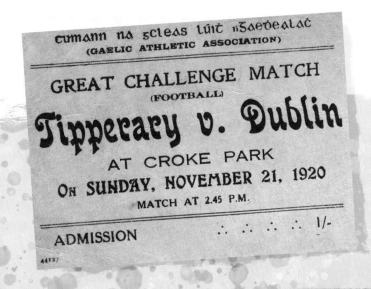

Michael Hogan

THE HOGAN STAND

Four years later, a new stand was named in memory of Michael Hogan. For many years, Bloody Sunday was commemorated on 21 November with a challenge game between Tipperary and Dublin. I witnessed a few of those matches, and they were always very moving occasions.

A TIME OF WAR

The War of Independence came, and then the Civil War, also known as Cogadh na gCarad (the War of Friends). Truly that was a dramatic period in Ireland's history, but the GAA managed to keep the championships going all through those years.

Éire Nua, Saorstát Éireann –
The Irish Free State

IRELAND AT THE OLYMPICS

In 1922, the twenty-six-county Irish Free State, Saorstát Éireann, was founded. This was a historic event for the people of Ireland and for Irish sport. Now 'Ireland' could take part in the Olympic Games, to be held in Paris in 1924.

The honour of carrying the Ireland flag into the Olympics went to the famous Kildare footballer Larry Stanley. He had already won All-Ireland medals with Kildare and Dublin, and was High Jump Champion of Ireland and Britain.

ARTS AT THE OLYMPICS

As well as sports, at that time the Olympics had competitions for the Arts. Jack B Yeats won a silver medal in Paris for his painting 'Swimming', while Oliver St John Gogarty earned a bronze for his poem 'Ode to the Tailteann Games'. These were Ireland's first Olympic medals.

Ardú meanman agus bród do mhuintir na h-Éireann a bhí ann gur thug siad boinn abhaile leo.

THE TAILTEANN GAMES

The Irish government decided to revive the ancient Tailteann Games to celebrate the birth of the new Irish Free State. The Tailteann Games were named after Queen Tailte, foster mother of Ireland's very first High King, Lugh Lámh Fhada – Lugh of the Long Arm.

The revived Games were held in Croke Park in 1924, soon after the end of the Olympics. They included many sports, such as running, jumping, hurling, football, camogie, spear throwing, sword-fighting, chariot and car racing. There was also singing, dancing, storytelling, craft competitions for goldsmiths, weavers and armourers and much more.

Anyone born in Ireland was allowed to compete, and many athletes who were in Paris for the Olympics that year came on to Dublin for the Games.

The games were a great success and a big boost for the 'new Ireland', and were held again in 1928 and 1932.

Thar aon rud eile chruthaigh Páirc an Chrócaigh go raibh an cumas ann ócáidí móra a reachtáil go beacht.

Stáisiún Raidió Saolaithe, Ó Domhnaill Abú agus Uile

The Saorstát Government had big plans for the development of the country, including the creation of a radio service. Ireland's first radio station, 2RN, went on air on 1 January 1926, launched by Douglas Hyde, a great champion of the Irish language who later became Ireland's first President.

LIVE FROM CROKE PARK

On 29 August 1926, Kilkenny and Galway were due to contest the All-Ireland Hurling Semi-Final in Croke Park. Leading up to the event, an employee of 2RN called PD Mehigan had an idea. He would commentate on the match as it happened, on the radio.

The GAA agreed, and so on match day, listeners all around the country were brought moment-by-moment commentary, live on air.

It was sensational.

PD Mehigan's live broadcast from Croke Park on that day was the first ever team sport to be broadcast live on any station in Europe, and one of the first in the whole world.

NEARLY LIVE FROM KILLARNEY

A builder's strike in 1937 meant that the Cusack Stand wasn't completed in time for that year's Hurling Final between Tipperary and Kilkenny. It was switched to Fitzgerald Stadium in Killarney.

Radio Éireann's commentary team of two was refused admission to the stadium, but they quickly found a solution – they bought tickets for admission and took turns running back and forth to the post office, where they broadcast from a telephone!

Necessity is the mother of invention after all.

KEEPING SCORE

Weeks later, the Cusack Stand was still not ready for the Cavan v Kerry Football Final. The fixture went ahead, but space for spectators was limited, and crowds were pushing and shoving to get in.

As tension grew in the exciting closing stages of the match, some spectators climbed up on to the scoreboard platform for a better view. In the chaos the scorekeeper was pushed aside, and the radio commentator mistakenly announced Cavan as one-point winners, when in fact the result was a draw!

'ADDED THRILLS'

Galway and Kerry clashed in the Football Final of 1938, and Michael Ó Hehir was there as commentator – his second match, and his first in Croke Park.

At half time, a man entered the 'box' wearing a balaclava and demanding to use the microphone.

Wisely, his wish was granted. He began to address the nation, and it was not a summary of the first half's play. He was disconnected before long, but his words had been heard across the country.

A newspaper headline the next morning said there were 'added thrills for listeners'.

Árdáin an Chrócaigh –
The Stands of Croke Park

THE HOGAN STAND

The first stand at Croke Park was built for the 1924 Tailteann Games. This was the Hogan Stand, along the west side of the pitch. Less than half the length of the pitch, it was named in memory of Michael Hogan who died on Bloody Sunday 1920.

When it was replaced in 1959, it was taken down and rebuilt at the Gaelic Grounds, Limerick.

THE CUSACK STAND

The second stand to make its appearance in Croke Park was named in memory of Michael Cusack, founder of the GAA in 1884.

Opened in 1938, the entire ground area from the Hill to the Canal had steps of cement and a good view of the pitch at all times. Above, supported by pillars, was seating for about 8,000 people.

The Cusack Stand gave some shelter from bad weather for those lucky enough to be under it.

THE DAVIN AND NALLY STANDS

In 1950, the Canal End terrace was opened, later named in memory of Maurice Davin, the first GAA President. Two years later, the Nally Stand was built in the corner between the Hogan Stand and the Hill, named in memory of Mayo man PW Nally, who died in Mountjoy Prison.

The old Nally Stand was eventually taken down and carefully re-erected in the GAA Grounds of Carrickmore, Co. Tyrone, in 2007.

REDEVELOPMENT

All was changed again when the entire stadium – pitch, dressing rooms, refreshment areas, offices, conference rooms and all the rest – was redesigned and rebuilt in the 1990s. The finished Croke Park is a real work of art, with one enormous roof stretching along three sides.

Today's Croke Park stadium has a capacity of 83,000, a crowd that raises quite a roar on big match days!

A NEW HOGAN STAND

By 1959, the seventy-fifth anniversary of the founding of the GAA, a magnificent new two-tier Hogan Stand stretched all along the western side of the Croke Park pitch. It was Ireland's first cantilever stand (with no pillars or supports to block the view), and had seats for 16,000 spectators.

HILL CULTURE

The fans who pack Dineen Hill 16 remained strongly in favour of keeping it as a roofless standing area. I was given a lovely phrase to explain this decision when I visited Shalke 04 Stadium in Germany a few years ago. I spotted an area almost exactly like Hill 16, and talked to a local about why it was kept this way. The answer was brief: 'Fan culture.'

Our own Dineen Hill 16 truly is a haven of culture.

Coirn Cumann Lúthchleas Gael – 'The Cups that Cheer'

Is dóigh liom-sa go bhfuil draíocht ag baint le coirn na gcluichí móra. Sé mo thuairim freisin go bhfuil an chumhacht acu daoine a chur faoi gheasa.

CORN MHIC CÁRTHAIGH – THE LIAM MACCARTHY CUP

This trophy is handed to the captain of the Senior All-Ireland winning hurling team.

Liam MacCarthy was born in London in 1853 to a Limerick mother and Cork father. He went on to become President of the London County GAA Board, and gave the GAA £50 to create a cup for the Senior All-Ireland hurling winners. It was crafted to look like a medieval drinking vessel.

The first team to lift the Cup was Limerick, when they defeated Dublin on 4 March 1923 in Croke Park in the delayed 1921 Final. Limerick captain Bob McConkey was the first to have the honour of raising it aloft.

The original Liam MacCarthy Cup was replaced in 1991 by a replica, which is still used today. Kilkenny have brought the famous 'Corn' home more times than any other county – 29 times between 1922 and 2015.

CORN SAM MAGUIDHIR – THE SAM MAGUIRE CUP

Sam Maguire was captain of the London Hibernians team that played in four All-Ireland finals – in 1900, 1901, 1902 and 1903 – but always came out second-best. Sam the man himself captained London on two of those occasions.

In 1907 he became chairman of London GAA (with vice-chairman Liam MacCarthy). The Cup named in his honour was raised for the first time in 1928 by the winning Kildare captain, Squires Gannon.

The 'Sam' is now rated the best-known trophy in Irish sport.

Go deimhin sé an sméar mhullaigh é.

The original cup was retired in 1988 and is now a 'resident' of the majestic Croke Park Museum. The new model, like the original, is modelled on the Ardagh Chalice. Kerry hold the record for Sam Maguire wins, with 30 in all between 1929 and 2014.

CORN UÍ DHUFAIGH –
THE O'DUFFY CUP

Like the Sam Maguire, the O'Duffy Cup is modelled on the Ardagh Chalice. It is presented to the captain of the All-Ireland Senior Camogie Championship winning team each year.

Seán O'Duffy was a member of Dublin club Kilmacud Crokes. He presented the trophy to the Camogie Association in 1932, the year that the Camogie Championships were introduced.

The first winners were Dublin, but the first camogie final to be held in Croke Park was that of 1934. A new replacement cup was presented for the first time in 2007.

The O'Duffy Cup has visited Cork more often than any other county, 28 times in all.

Nach iontach an radharc é le cúpla bliain anuas breis agus 50,000 de lucht leanta le feiscint ag Cluichí móra na mBan.

CORN BREANDÁN Ó MÁIRTÍN –
THE BRENDAN MARTIN CUP

The Brendan Martin Cup is presented to the captain of the All-Ireland winning team in the Ladies' Senior Football Championship.

Brendan was an Offaly man who helped organise the newly-formed Ladies' Gaelic Football Association in the 1970s.

The Cup was first awarded to Tipperary, who beat Offaly in the 1974 Championship. The game was played in Durrow, Co. Laois.

The Brendan Martin Cup was held aloft in Croke Park for the first time when Kerry beat Wexford in the final of 1986.

Kerry and Cork are level with 11 victories each since the cup was first presented in 1974.

The County Colours

CONNACHT

Galway: The Tribesmen
County colours: maroon, white

Leitrim: The O'Rourke County
County colours: green, gold

Mayo: The Westerns
County colours: green, red

Roscommon: The Rossies
County colours: yellow, blue

Sligo: The Yeats County
County colours: black, white

LEINSTER

Carlow: The Barrowsiders
County colours: green, red, yellow

Dublin: The Dubs / The Jackeens / The Boys in
Blue / The Liffeysiders
County colours: sky blue, navy

Kildare: The Lilywhites
County colours: white

Kilkenny: The Cats
County colours: black, amber

Laois: The O'Moore County
County colours: blue, white

Longford: Midlanders
County colours: royal blue, gold

Louth: The Wee County
County colours: red, white

Meath: The Royals
County colours: green, gold

Offaly: The Faithful County
County colours: green, white, gold

Westmeath: The Lake County
County colours: maroon, white

Wexford: The Model County
County colours: purple, gold

Wicklow: The Garden County
County colours: blue, yellow

MUNSTER

Clare: The Banner
County colours: yellow, blue

Cork: The Rebels
County colours: red, white

Kerry: The Kingdom
County colours: green, gold

Limerick: The Shannonsiders
County colours: green, white

Tipperary: The Premier County
County colours: blue, yellow

Waterford: The Déise
County colours: white, blue

ULSTER

Antrim: The Glensmen
County colours: yellow, white

Armagh: The Orchard County
County colours: orange, white

Cavan: The Breifne County
County colours: blue, white

Derry: The Oakleaf County
County colours: red, white

Donegal: The Tír Chonaill men
County colours: green, gold

Down: The Mournemen (football) /
The Ardsmen (hurling)
County colours: red, black

Fermanagh: The Ernesiders
County colours: green, white

Monaghan: The Oriel County /
The Farney Army
County colours: white, blue

Tyrone: The O'Neill County /
The Red Hands
County colours: white, red

Cluichí Spreagúla i bPáirc an Chrócaigh – Memorable Games in Croke Park – Football

Does anybody ever forget the first All-Ireland Final they witnessed?

Bhuel, níl mise ina measc pé scéal é. Ní baol go ndéanfaidh mé dearmad air go lá Pilib a' Chleite!

There are many other matches that I will never forget, one of them in 1960.

THE ALL-IRELAND FOOTBALL FINAL OF 1960

This match was historic with a capital H.

Kerry were reigning All-Ireland Champions, by then having won the title nineteen times. Down had qualified for their first All-Ireland Final. Of course, Kerry were raging favourites to win, with Down venturing into an unknown arena.

So it was a shock to spectators when the Down men operated like seasoned stars almost from the beginning. They were eight points ahead when the final whistle sounded, clearly the better team.

The on-field celebrations were the greatest ever witnessed, and it was generally accepted that Down were very worthy winners.

Preparations then began for the first journey of the Sam Maguire Cup across the 'Border' for the first time.

The Down men were a team of very fine footballers. They bagged two more titles before the decade was out, and were an inspiration to all the counties of Ulster.

Since then, Ulster counties Armagh, Tyrone, Donegal and Derry have all taken Sam Maguire home.

Tá an caighdeán peile i gCúige Uladh chun tosaigh go mór ar na cúigí eile faoi láthair.

Ar chuala sibh riamh faoi Chluiche Ceannais Peile 1982?

Is there anybody who did not? It was Ciarraí v Uibh Fháilí, with Kerry in hot pursuit of the elusive five in a row of All-Ireland titles. Before that, two teams had started a season with a four-in-a-row badge, but neither had managed to reach the Final.

Was it the greatest game of Gaelic Football ever played? It has good claim to that title. The end of the match was probably the most dramatic ever, with Seamus Darby's last-minute goal denying the Kingdom their five in a row.

The game was also a magnificent display of Gaelic football, played as football should be played. The standard was stellar, and the epic story will live forever and a day.

An mbeidh a leithéid arís ann?

A Great Rivalry – Kerry vs Dublin

Few All-Irelands could compare with the finals of 1955 and 1975, with Kerry against Dublin on both occasions. The atmosphere in the lead-up to both matches was truly memorable, particularly the 1955 game.

There was a craving for an All-Ireland win by Dublin in the early 1950s, and the team was looking like a good or maybe a great one.

Dublin had won 14 All-Irelands between 1891 and 1923, including winning three in a row three times. However, between 1924 and 1958 Dublin had only won the All-Ireland title once, beating Galway in 1942.

Now, in 1955, Dublin had won the League, beating reigning All-Ireland champions Meath by 12 points. A dozen of the Dublin players were from the great St Vincent's Club.

The Leinster Championship was next, and the Leinster Final scoreboard read Dublin 5-12 , Meath 0-7.

Both All-Ireland Semi-finals – Dublin/Mayo and Kerry/Cavan – ended in draws. The replays were held on the same day, and the atmosphere was that of an unending carnival.

Kerry and Dublin qualified for the All-Ireland Final, attracting 87,102 spectators. This time, thirteen from the St Vincent's Club played for Dublin. Only three points separated the sides at the finish: Kerry 0-12, Dublin 1-6.

Throughout the 1970s, rivalry was again fierce between Kerry and Dublin. In 1975, Dublin were defending champions and strong favourites for the 'double'. However, an extremely young Kerry side managed by Mick O'Dwyer played brilliantly and claimed the title.

Kevin Heffernan was the Dublin 'manager', a new word in Gaelic lore at the time. It was the same pairing for the 1976 Final, and the usual great expectations abounded. Heffo's team played brilliantly, scored three goals and won by 7 points.

Kevin Heffernan announced his retirement soon after, and team captain Tony Hanahoe succeeded the maestro.

Fate brought the sides together in the Semi-Final of 1977, in what may have been the greatest game of Gaelic Football ever played. With a level of speed and determination rarely seen, two spectacular goals close to the end earned Dublin a very sweet victory on that day.

Neither side has been 'away' for long. After losing out in 1977, Mick O'Dwyer's team won four in a row. Then, after a gap of two years, they added a three in a row.

And who will ever forget Dublin's capture of the first ever five in a row in All-Ireland history in the captivating atmosphere of historic September 2019?

May we see its like again.

Memorable Games in Croke Park – Ladies' Football

Back in the 1980s, Kerry's Ladies' Football team was unbeatable – literally! With star players like Mary Jo Curran and Margaret Lawlor, they won every All-Ireland Final from 1982 to 1990. In 1990, they beat Laois 1-9 to 0-6, to complete an amazing nine in a row.

Theip ar Chiarraí san Ath-Bhliain nuair bhí an bua ag Port Láirge in a n-aghaidh.

Waterford went on to beat Laois in the final. Aine Wall was the star for the Munster side, scoring 3 goals and 7 points to help her county to a 5-8 to 3-7 win. The match equalled the record for the highest number of goals scored in a football final.

Laois lost no less than seven All-Ireland finals between 1985 and 1996. Then, in 2001, they faced Mayo in a gruelling and nail-biting final. Scores were level, with just a few seconds left, when Laois were awarded a free. Mary Kirwan took the free, scoring the winning point with the very last kick of the game, ending decades of disappointment for Laois.

In the first of three finals in a row featuring Cork and Dublin, 2014 was a real thriller. With eight All-Ireland titles in nine years under their belts, Cork were surprised to find themselves a massive ten points down to Dublin, 0-6 to 2-10, with just fifteen minutes to go. But an impressive comeback, with subs Rhona Ní Bhuachalla and Eimear Scally scoring a goal each, saw the Rebels clinch victory by one point two minutes from the final whistle.

Ladies' Football is of a high standard at the moment, and has a massive following.

Memorable Games in Croke Park – Hurling

Is hurling the greatest game played in Ireland? The answer is a definite 'yes'. I have watched quite a few matches over the years and have marvelled at the skills on display.

Each of the six counties of Munster have won a Senior All-Ireland Hurling Championship. Surprisingly, only five of Leinster's twelve counties have achieved the honour. No Ulster team has ever succeeded, and only Galway has made the grade in Connacht.

The Cork hurlers won four All-Ireland Championships between 1941 and '44, but the run ended there.

The National League Final of 1956 was a truly epic game of hurling, as Wexford came from fourteen points down at half time to beat Tipperary by four. The hurling was good, hard and fast, and it still registers in many memories.

Wexford beat a highly rated Cork side by six points in the fantastic All-Ireland Hurling Final of the same year. With the end not far away, Cork were applying huge pressure and a goal would have edged them in front.

The legendary Christy Ring's effort for a goal was blocked by Slaneyside goalkeeper Art Foley, and the sliothar was cleared by Mick Morrissey. Amid a torrent of sound that could only have come from the heavens, the move ended in a goal for Wexford and a wonderful victory.

After the final whistle, rather than rush towards colleagues to celebrate, Wexford defenders Nick O'Donnell and Bobby Rackard hoisted Cork's warrior, Christy Ring, onto their shoulders. It was a most noble gesture in honour of the Corkman, holder of eight All-Ireland medals and in his sixteenth year of service to Cork. What a memorable and magnificent moment. I shall never forget it.

OFFALY HURLING

'*Is fánach an áit in a bhfaighfeá breac*' – one can catch a trout in an unusual place.

The story of Offaly Hurling during the last twenty years of the twentieth century is nothing short of miraculous. Before capturing their first Leinster title in 1980, they had contested only one since 1928. And yet from 1980, they played in eleven consecutive Leinster Finals, capturing the title seven times.

With four All-Ireland titles – in 1981, 1985, 1994 and 1998 – the question of divine inspiration surfaces.

Nobody could have foreseen even a hint of it, and so that Offaly era deserves a place of honour in our memories.

THE CATS

Kilkenny heads the order of merit, with a wonderful haul of 36 Senior All-Ireland titles. I watched them win 23 of those titles, and often wonder which was the best of them all in the memories of Kilkenny folk.

Perhaps the defeat of Tipperary in the 1967 final was the sweetest, as it was the first win over their great rivals since 1922. John Doyle, Tipperary's warrior defender, was going for his ninth All-Ireland medal that day, but the Cats were in a zone that could only produce a win.

Tipp were equally brilliant in that decade, winning 4 All-Irelands.

In the years 1958–68, Tipperary won five All-Irelands and five National Leagues. I never thought I would see a team surpass that Tipperary side.

But I now grant a slight edge to the valiant Kilkenny, who won five National League titles and seven All-Irelands, including four in a row, in a decade of success from 2000 to 2009. It will take a team of heroes to dislodge the Cats.

In 2009, Kilkenny's opponents were Tipperary, and the pace, passion, intensity and skill were awe-inspiring.

I can still see Kilkenny defender Michael Kavanagh racing from the Canal End in pursuit of a rolling sliothar heading for the Hogan side-line. Meanwhile Tipperary's roaming forward Lar Corbett approaches rapidly from an outfield area. By a split second, Kavanagh gets there first. He manages to hold the sliothar inside the line, leading to a goal for the Cats and their four-in-a-row victory.

Unforgettable – only one blade of grass between victory and defeat.

Let us salute both sets of Cú Chulainns.

Memorable Games in Croke Park – Camogie

The 1955 Camogie Final between rivals Dublin and Cork was one of the greatest in history. Cork took the lead in the opening minutes, but were trailing Dublin 3-2 to 1-4 at half-time. The closing score was 9-2 to 5-6, with goals scored by Dublin's brilliant Sophie Brack, her colleague Frances Maher (who accounted for 6) and Cork's Noreen Duggan.

In 1973, Cork took on Antrim in their quest for four in a row. Ann Phelan's goal for Cork came just three minutes before full-time, and Marion McCarthy's point two minutes later seemed to put an end to the contest.

But Antrim were not surrendering without a fight. Captain Mairéad McAtamney soon smashed the sliothar into the back of the Cork net, leaving just one point between the teams in the dying seconds of the game. Cork doggedly managed to hold on to win 2-5 to 3-1.

Cork's junior team were victorious that same day and Cally Riordan, who played in both finals, became the only person to win two All-Ireland medals in one day.

In 1999, Tipperary's rising star Claire Grogan became the youngest player to line out for her county in an All-Ireland Final since the 1950s – she was just 14 years of age. Before long Claire was winning medals, and won no less than 5 All-Ireland medals in six years. She also had great success with her club, Cashel, and captained them to All-Ireland glory in 2009.

2012 produced a thrilling final, with Wexford against Cork, seeking three in a row. Wexford ended as victors, with Ursula Jacob contributing 2 goals and 7 points.

Two Cork players, Briege Corkery and Rena Buckley, also played on that year's All-Ireland-winning Ladies' Football team.

Weird and Wonderful Games From History

The Senior All-Ireland Hurling Final of 1901 was not played until 1903.

Cork, represented by the Redmonds, lined out in Jones' Road against a London selection as follows: 9 Cork-born, 4 from Limerick and 1 each from Tipperary and Kerry.

The final score was London 1-5, Cork 0-4. No overseas team has won an All-Ireland since.

Edward Barrett, the London Kerryman, later won Olympic Games medals representing Britain.

Another wandering Kerry player, Jackie Flavin, lined out for Galway Footballers in the All-Ireland final of 1938. He wore the number 10 jersey when defeating Kerry in the Final.

Strangely, he had also worn the number 10 jersey a year earlier when winning an All-Ireland medal as a member of the Kerry team.

Bobby Beggs, a fisherman from Skerries in Dublin, was another noted footballer and traveller. He won a Railway Cup medal with his province Leinster in 1935.

When fishing was not going well he went to work in Galway. He won a Railway Cup medal with Connacht in 1936, another in '37 and an All-Ireland medal as a centre-back with Galway a year later.

On returning to Dublin, he was soon back on his native county team. He played on the winning 1942 team, defeating Galway in the Final.

Kerrymen occupied three of the four midfield berths in that final – Joe Fitzgerald (captain) and Michael Falvey for Dublin, and Dan Kavanagh for Galway. Dublin also included Paddy Henry of Sligo, Caleb Crone of Cork and J Joy of Kerry.

Strange times indeed.

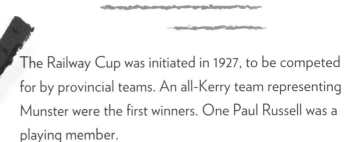

The Railway Cup was initiated in 1927, to be competed for by provincial teams. An all-Kerry team representing Munster were the first winners. One Paul Russell was a playing member.

He was chosen again for the 1928 Munster side, but a little problem surfaced – the Leinster selectors also selected him. The Central Council of the GAA ruled that he should play for Leinster. He did, and won his second Railway Cup medal.

Also in the Railway Cup, on St Patrick's Day of 1962, 21-year-old Des Foley of Dublin played at midfield for the full length of the Hurling and Football finals in Croke Park. Leinster won both.

Des was out on the golf course early the next morning for a round of golf and a bit of fresh air.

My All Star

Players of all generations have considered it a great honour to play in Croke Park. If I had to pick one that I found the most inspiring it would be a man I had the good fortune to meet on many occasions.

Frank or Fergus Burke, or Proinsias De Búrca, was born in Kildare in 1895.

In boarding school at Knockbeg College in Carlow, he made sure he brought along his trusty hurl. He was disappointed to discover that cricket was the College's game.

During the summer holidays that followed, he discovered from a poster in a shop window in Rathfarnham that a school existed that encouraged hurling. This was Scoil Éanna, founded by none other than the nationalist leader Padraig Pearse. Frank opted for that scoil at once. He studied and played, and later returned as a qualified teacher to work at Scoil Éanna.

He joined the Irish Republican Brotherhood to fight against British rule, and was a founder member of the Irish Volunteers in 1913. During the Easter Rising of 1916 he was in Dublin's GPO and then manned a barricade on Moore Street. He was imprisoned in Britain.

After his release, he went back to teaching at Scoil Éanna and back to hurling and football. One of the most successful dual players of all time, he appeared for Dublin in no less than nine All-Ireland Finals, winning three in Football and two in Hurling.

On Bloody Sunday, he was the Dublin player marking Tipperary's Michael Hogan.

De Burca's last game for Dublin was in the 1927 Championships.

He lived until his 93rd year, in 1987. His story and those of his comrades will live forever.

Bhí sé dílis go bás do chultúr uilig na h-Éireann agus bhain sé taitneamh do-chreidte as gach gné de.

Mar a deireann an t-amhrán – Sé mo laoch, mo ghile mear.